A B C
PASTA

An Entertaining Alphabet

Juana Medina

viking

Aa

angel hair acrobats

Bb

basil balancing ballerinas

campanelle clowns

Cc

Dd

ditalini daredevils

egg noodle equilibrists

Ee

Ff

fettuccine fire-eaters

gemelli gymnasts

Gg

herb hoops

Hh

I i

invincible integrale Ingrid

linguini leotard Lois

Ll

Mm

Macaroni the magician

Nn

nero di seppia nets

Oo

orzo orchestra

Pp

Pecorino and Parmigiano, plate spinners

Qq

quick Quentin quadrucci

rigatoni ringmaster

Rr

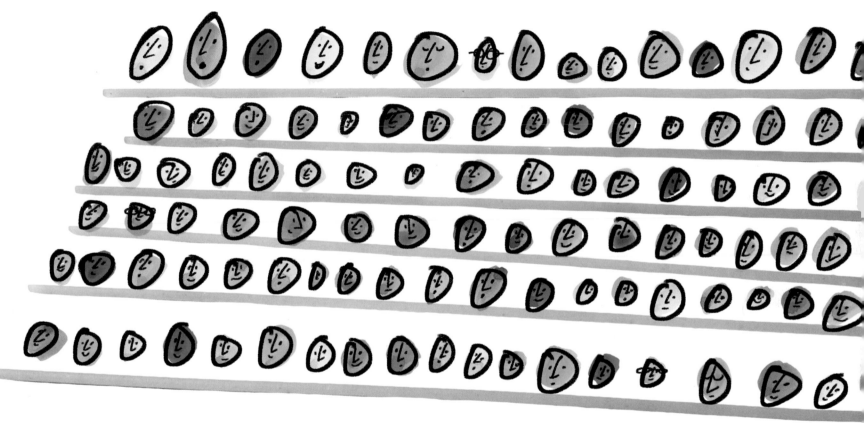

spaghetti spectators

Tt

tortellini trapeze trio

all'uovo unicycler

Uu

Vv

vermicelli vanishing act

wonder wagon wheels

Ww

X x

x-traordinary Xavier the xylophonist

Yy

yolk-less pasta yodelers

zestful zip liner ziti

Zz

Acrobats, Ballerinas,

Clowns, and more!

To Miss Marielita *for teaching me the ABCs.*

Viking

Penguin Young Readers Group

An imprint of Penguin Random House LLC

375 Hudson Street

New York, New York 10014

First published in the United States of America by Viking,

an imprint of Penguin Random House LLC, 2017

LIBRARY OF CONGRESS CATALOGING-IN-PUBLICATION DATA IS AVAILABLE.

ISBN 9781101999783

1 3 5 7 9 10 8 6 4 2

Manufactured in China   Book design by Nancy Brennan   Set in Bodoni Six and Burbank big wide

The artwork was made using digital illustration and photographs of a variety of pastas, herbs, and cheeses.

Cacio e Pepe

1½ cups grated pecorino

1 cup grated parmigiano

Black pepper to taste

Coarse salt

1 lb pasta

Cook pasta al dente.

While pasta cooks, combine cheese and black pepper in a large bowl.

Add just enough pasta water to make a thick paste.

Drain pasta, add to bowl, and mix together.

Top with extra pecorino and pepper. Enjoy!